Contents

Ni hao!   5

Lands of the south   6

On top of the world   8

Sichuan to Shanghai   10

Yellow earth   12

The far north   14

Beijing   16

All in a day's work   18

At home   20

Leisure and the arts   22

China long ago   24

The Middle Kingdom   26

New worlds   28

Fact file   30

Index   32

4

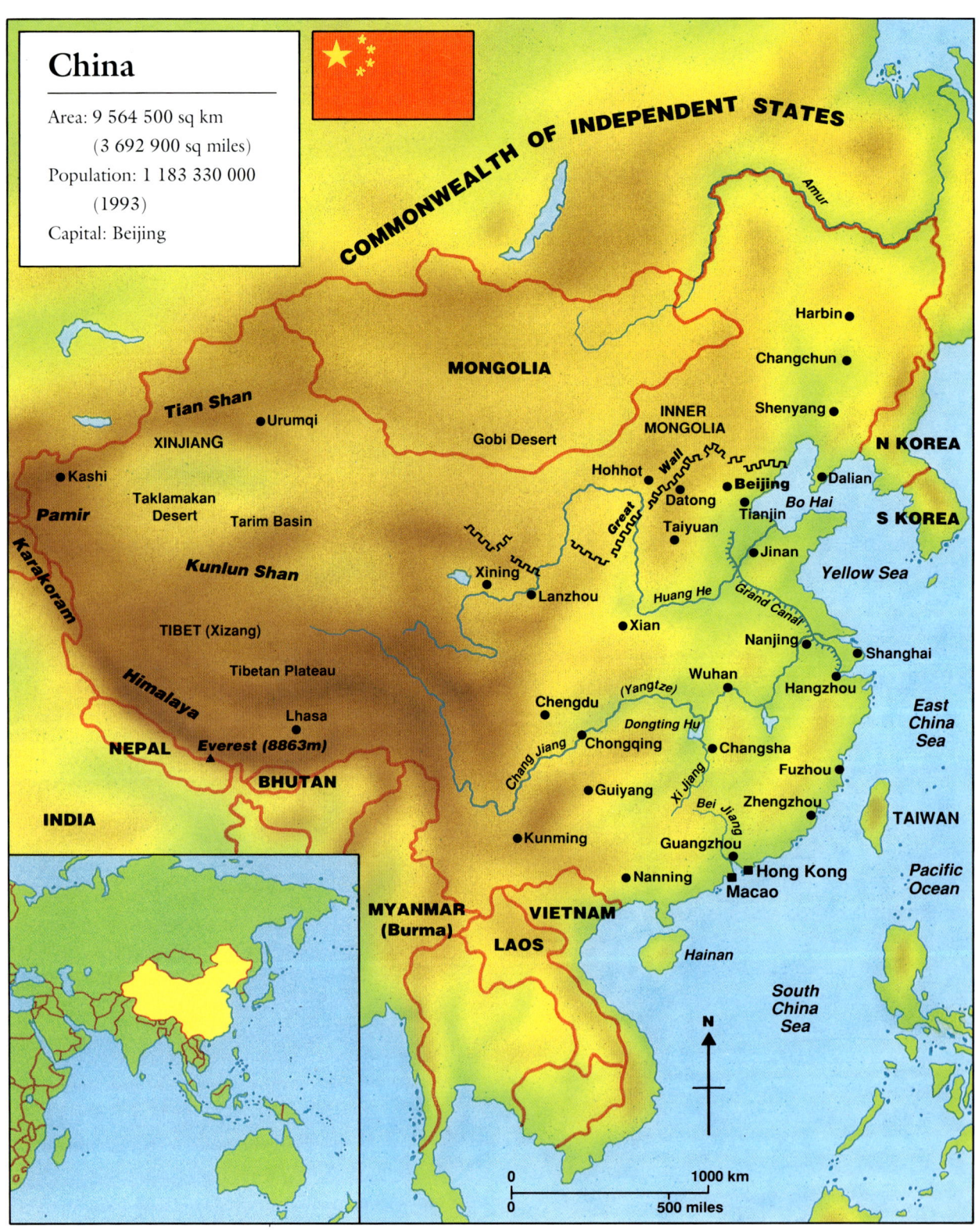

China

Area: 9 564 500 sq km
(3 692 900 sq miles)

Population: 1 183 330 000
(1993)

Capital: Beijing

COMMONWEALTH OF INDEPENDENT STATES

Amur

MONGOLIA

Harbin ●
Changchun ●
Shenyang ●

INNER
MONGOLIA

N KOREA

Tian Shan
Urumqi ●

XINJIANG

Gobi Desert

Hohhot ●

Great Wall

Beijing ●
Datong ●

Dalian ●

Bo Hai

S KOREA

Kashi ●

Pamir

Taklamakan
Desert

Tarim Basin

Taiyuan ●

Tianjin ●

Jinan ●

Yellow Sea

Karakoram

Kunlun Shan

Xining ●

Lanzhou ●

Huang He

Grand Canal

Xian ●

Nanjing ●

Shanghai ●

TIBET (Xizang)

Tibetan Plateau

Wuhan ●

Hangzhou ●

East
China
Sea

Himalaya

Lhasa ●

Everest (8863m) ▲

NEPAL

BHUTAN

Chengdu ●

(Yangtze)

Dongting Hu

Chang Jiang

Chongqing ●

Changsha ●

Fuzhou ●

Zhengzhou ●

INDIA

Guiyang ●

Xi Jiang

Bei Jiang

TAIWAN

Kunming ●

Guangzhou ●

Nanning ●

Hong Kong ■
Macao

Pacific
Ocean

MYANMAR
(Burma)

VIETNAM

LAOS

Hainan

South
China
Sea

N

Ni hao! 你好

This greeting may be heard all over the People's Republic of China. '*Ni hao!*' means 'Hello!' in the Chinese language sometimes called Mandarin. This is the language most Chinese children learn in school. There are many other local versions of the Chinese language, such as Cantonese. This is spoken around Guangzhou, in the far south of the country.

Other languages are also to be heard, for China is home to many different peoples. The largest group of people is the Han Chinese, but there are 56 other groups, including Tibetans, Mongols, Zhuang, Hui and Miao.

A vast nation

More people live in China than in any other country on earth. The population is over one thousand million people! The east and south of the country are very crowded, but the far west and north include vast desert and mountain regions where few people can live.

China is a huge land. It is nearly as large as the continent of Europe and it shares land borders with 14 other nations. To the north lie the snowy forests of Siberia, in Russia. To the south lie the tropical lands of India and Southeast Asia.

The Yellow Sea and the East and South China Seas are part of the Pacific Ocean. Ocean winds bring heavy seasonal rains and storms called typhoons

A Miao girl dresses up in the traditional costume of her people.

to these coasts.

China is divided into five regions, 22 provinces and three city areas called municipalities.

Lands of the south

China's southeast is an area of great beauty. There are mountains, hills and plains, yellow with flowering rape and green with bamboo. The climate is warm and moist, making it possible to grow large amounts of rice and tea. There is fishing along the coasts.

Some of the industries in the area have been there for hundreds of years. Hangzhou is known for its silk. Jingdezhen produces fine china, called porcelain. In Fuzhou, wood is coloured and varnished to make beautiful lacquer furniture.

There are modern industries too, such as electronics and chemicals. Guangdong province has become a centre of business, with skyscrapers rising above the cities of Shantou, Shenzhen and Zhuhai.

The biggest city of the south is Guangzhou or Canton, a modern city full of people, buses and bicycles. It is known around the world for its style of cooking. The surrounding countryside produces lush fruit such as pineapples and lychees.

Ferries from Guangzhou's riverside quays take passengers south to blue seas, where flying fish skim the waves. The tropical beaches of Hainan Island are being developed for tourism.

Many tourists visit Guangxi region, which is the home of the Zhuang people. At Guilin they see a river landscape which looks as though it comes from an ancient Chinese painting. Tall rocks rise from the misty waters of the Xi Jiang.

The peaceful waters of Guilin, one of the most beautiful scenes in southern China

The limestone pillars of Shilin, in Yunnan

The land of spring

The province of Yunnan lies in the southwest of China. Yunnan is home to the Yi and the Dai peoples. A railway, passing by rocky gorges and rushing rivers, leads to the large city of Kunming. This city lies at the northern end of a beautiful lake. In Kunming there are wide modern streets and green parks with flowers and goldfish ponds. The climate is fresh and pleasant.

From here you can travel by bus to the strange landscape of Shilin, the Stone Forest. It takes its name from tall pillars of grey limestone. A longer journey takes you westwards to the foothills of the Himalayas, or southwards to the tropical forests of Xishuangbanna, home to rare tigers and peacocks.

Communist or capitalist?

China has been governed by Communists since 1949. At first, its factories and farms were run by the state but there have been many changes in recent years. Foreign firms have been allowed to set up businesses in China. Farmers have been able to sell their goods on the private market. Even so, the economy is still not run in a capitalist way, as it would be in Europe or America.

Parts of southern China have been ruled by capitalists during the period since 1949. The independent island of Taiwan has been governed by Chinese nationalists, who were against communism. Macao, the most crowded piece of land in the world, is governed by the Portuguese. It will be returned to China in 1999. The British colony of Hong Kong, a centre of international trade and banking, will be returned to China in 1997.

Hong Kong's harbour is lined with skyscrapers.

On top of the world

China's southwestern border is guarded by the world's highest mountains. The snowy peak of Mount Everest, known to the Chinese as Qomolangma, soars to a height of 8863 m (29 078 ft).

The huge area of the Tibetan plateau is sometimes called 'the roof of the world'. The plateau is a lonely world of icy mountain passes, where people herd yaks, the shaggy oxen of the Himalayas. There are Buddhist temples and remote villages.

The region of Tibet (Xizang in Chinese) has its own language, history and traditions. Tibet has at times been recognised as an independent country,

The Potala towers above the city of Lhasa.

A horse and cart on the old 'Silk Road'

and today many Tibetans would like to govern themselves. Many people have left Tibet for Nepal and India, where their religious leader, the Dalai Lama, lives in exile. His former palace, the Potala, is in the city of Lhasa.

The Silk Road

For thousands of years camels and mules have picked their way through the empty deserts and mountain valleys of northwest China. The beasts were once laden high with bales of Chinese silk and with tea, pressed into solid bricks. Merchants risked attack by bandits as they travelled westwards to sell their goods in Persia, Arabia and Europe.

Today, buses and trucks drive through this harsh landscape. A rough highway has been built through the Karakoram mountains. It goes all the way to Pakistan.

The northwest

Tajiks and Uzbeks live in the mountains and deserts of the Xinjiang region. These people speak languages which sound like Turkish, and they follow the Islamic faith.

The northwestern landscape is bleak and hostile. In summer the temperature can rise to 48°C (118°F). However irrigation has brought water from the mountains to this wilderness, making it possible to grow fruit and grain crops. In recent years, oil and precious metals have been discovered in Xinjiang, and this is bringing further changes to the region.

Followers of Islam are called to prayer in Kashgar.

Sichuan to Shanghai

In the province of Sichuan, large areas of the mountain slopes are covered by bamboo. The bamboo is food for the giant panda. This habitat is being threatened by humans, but special reserves have been set aside to protect the panda's future.

The mountains of Sichuan are cool and misty for much of the year. They border a large plain. The industrial city of Chengdu lies on this rich farmland.

The rivers of Sichuan drain into the Chang Jiang. This is the world's third biggest river, with a length of about 6300km (3937 miles). A stretch of it is called the Yangtze. When Europeans came to China, they gave this name to the whole river.

Chongqing is the largest city in Sichuan. It has many factories and their

Giant pandas live in the mountains of southwest China.

River traffic passes through the Gezhouba lock.

chimneys pollute the air. From here you can take a crowded river steamer, eastwards down the Chang Jiang. The river is busy with shipping, from barges loaded with coal to small boats carrying local produce.

From Chongqing the river flows eastwards, rushing through deep, rocky gorges. The force of the water drives the turbines of the huge Gezhouba Dam hydroelectric scheme. The river steamers have to pass through a great lock to reach the lower part of the river. Here the Chang Jiang becomes broad and sluggish. It flows on through the farmland of Hunan and Hubei. This is a rice and cotton growing area. There are also many large cities. Passengers leave the steamer at Wuhan. Some of them take a train from here, north to Beijing or south to Guangzhou. Others can board another ship and continue downstream towards Shanghai.

A north-south link

The rice-growing lands around the lower Chang Jiang are linked to the north of the country by *Da Yunhe*, the Grand Canal. Work on this began in 540 BC and it was completed in AD 1327. As many as five million people worked on this great engineering project. The southern section, which starts at Hangzhou, is still busy with shipping today. Mud has silted up the northern end of the canal.

Shanghai

The Chang Jiang reaches the East China Sea near the great port of Shanghai, on the Huangpu River. There are buildings in the European style along the waterfront, or Bund. During the 1800s and early 1900s the city was controlled by foreign powers.

Today Shanghai is China's largest city with a population of nearly 13 million. There are shipyards and steelworks in Shanghai, and factories producing televisions and other household goods.

The bright lights of Shanghai

Yellow earth

The flooding waters of the Huang He carry thick mud downstream.

To the north of the Chang Jiang valley there is a great plateau. The winters here are bitterly cold and the summers hot and dusty. Earthquakes are frequent in this region.

The type of yellow-brown soil found in this area is known as loess. Over thousands of years, this soil has been carried to the region by winds blowing from the deserts which lie further north. Trees have to be planted to keep the soil stable. The loess is good for growing vegetables and grain crops such as wheat, maize and sorghum.

Another great river winds its way through these central northern provinces. This river is the Huang He, or Yellow River. The river's course has changed many times over the ages. Because of disastrous floods, the river became known as 'China's sorrow'.

The flow of the river is now controlled by dams, and banks of earth called levees. Ditches were also dug to help to control the floods. Some of these ditches have become silted up with the thick, yellow-brown mud that gave the river its name. The same floods that once brought misery to northern farmers also brought them this rich, muddy soil for cultivation.

Northern cities

In many northern cities ancient and modern buildings stand side by side. Xi'an, in Shaanxi province, was once the capital of China. It still has many features of an ancient Chinese town, with high city walls, tall towers and pagodas and ancient tombs. There is a Grand Mosque here, a centre for Islam in China. Xi'an is surrounded by factories and textile mills and has a population of over 2.7 million.

The northern provinces produce coal, iron and steel, and manufacture trucks, machinery, carpets and household goods.

The port for the central northern provinces is Tianjin, on the eastern gulf of Bo Hai. This city is home to some eight million people – about twice the population of Norway.

Steel being made in the blast furnace

A steam locomotive waits at the platform.

Travel by rail

The town of Datong, in Shanxi province, still manufactures steam engines. These powerful locomotives may still be seen puffing their way across China, although most Chinese trains are now hauled by diesel power.

It is possible to take a diesel express all the way from China to Moscow, the capital of Russia. The journey takes six days!

Few Chinese people own cars, so rail travel is a very important form of transport. The cheapest tickets are for very crowded carriages. More expensive tickets buy seats, bunks or sleepers.

On the train, attendants bring flasks of hot water, for everybody likes to brew their own mug of tea. Take-away food can be bought in small disposable boxes or meals may be eaten in the restaurant car. Snacks are sold on station platforms.

The far north

The Mongol people live in the region of Inner Mongolia, alongside many Han Chinese who have settled there. Mongols also live in Russia and across the border in the independent country of Mongolia. Seven hundred years ago the Mongol empire stretched all the way to Europe. The Mongol people have their own languages and customs, and traditionally they follow the Buddhist faith.

Inner Mongolia is a wide, grassy plateau. It borders the sandy dunes of the Gobi Desert. Shaggy, two-humped Bactrian camels are the main form of transport in the desert. Inner Mongolia is freezing cold in winter and extremely hot in summer.

The Mongol people are expert horse riders. They raise camels, sheep, goats and cattle. Some Mongols are nomads, wandering the grasslands with their herds. They live in large, round tents made of warm felt. This kind of tent is called a *ger* or a *yurt*.

Many Mongols have now given up the wandering life and settled down in villages and towns. Cities such as Hohhot and Baotou have grown very quickly and there are now tall blocks of flats, factories and steelworks.

Rounding up herds in the Mongolian grasslands

The northeast

Between the gulf of Bo Hai and the Amur River lie the provinces of Liaoning, Jilin and Heilongjiang. This part of China used to be known as Manchuria. The winters here are icy, but in the summer there are large harvests of sugar beet, millet, maize, sunflower seed and soya beans. Soya is used in many Chinese dishes.

The central plain is bordered by two mountain ranges called the Greater and Lesser Hinggan. Much of the region is covered in forests, which provide timber. Coal, iron and copper are mined and oil is drilled at Daqing. The northeast has become one of China's most important industrial centres, producing cars and trucks, paper and chemicals.

Carpenters using timber to build a house

Protected wildlife – the Japanese crane

In the wilds

The northeastern provinces are home to the brown bear, the red deer and the lynx. One of its rarest animals is the Manchurian tiger, the largest member of the cat family. Bird life includes beautiful long-legged cranes.

Much of China is very crowded, and people are everywhere. There are few wild animals which are not hunted or scared away. In more remote areas, China still has a fascinating variety of wildlife. However even here there are problems, as forests are cut down and new villages are built. Many rare animals are threatened.

To protect the future of its wildlife, China has created over 330 nature reserves. The largest of these is Changbaishan, in Jilin.

Beijing

China's capital city, Beijing (also called Peking), is in the north of the country. Nearly 11 million people live here – and most of them seem to ride bicycles! Thousands of cyclists wait at busy road junctions. There are also taxis, mini-vans and private cars, packed buses, horses and carts – and a modern underground railway.

The Palace of Heavenly Purity is part of Beijing's ancient Forbidden City.

The old city was once a maze of narrow alleyways. Today, many of these have been cleared to make way for broad streets, high-rise flats and luxury hotels.

The Imperial Palace is at the centre of the city. In the old days, Chinese emperors lived here in luxury. Ordinary

Bicycles, buses and bustle in the modern city

people were not allowed to enter the palace or its huge grounds, so it became known as the Forbidden City. The public can now visit the palace and see the splendid wooden buildings and courtyards behind the high red walls.

In front of the palace is the world's biggest square, Tiananmen. It was here, in 1949, that the communist leader Mao Zedong, announced that China would become a People's Republic.

The centre of government

Beijing is the centre of the government and the ruling Communist Party. The National People's Congress, which makes laws, is elected for a term of five years.

The municipalities of Beijing, Tianjin and Shanghai are ruled directly from Beijing. The provinces have their own congresses and send representatives to Beijing. The regions are said to be autonomous, or self-governing.

Sights to see

From **Tiananmen Square** you can visit the Great Hall of the People, the tomb of Mao Zedong and the Monument to the Heroes.

Beihai Park lies to the northwest of the Forbidden City. Beneath its *dagoba*, a Buddhist monument from 300 years ago, are pavilions, paths, and lakes used for boating and skating.

Tiantan is the Temple of Heaven, built in 1420. This was where the emperors used to pray each year for a good harvest. It is one of the finest buildings in China.

The **Yonghe Lamasery** has been a religious centre since 1723, although it was closed during the 1950s and 1960s. People come here to see its Buddhist shrines.

The **Summer Palace** is one of the most beautiful sites in Beijing, set amongst lakes and hills.

The splendid roof of Tiantan, the Temple of Heaven

All in a day's work

Women work in the flooded rice fields of Kangsu.

China has many hungry mouths to feed. Chinese farmers must cultivate all the land available, even in regions where the landscape makes farming difficult.

It is hard work. Labourers in the sugar-cane fields and flooded rice paddies of the south wear broad-brimmed hats of straw or cotton to keep off the heat of the sun. In the cold northern winters, workers must wear thick padded jackets to keep out the cold.

Vast amounts of food are produced, even though most people are poor and farm machinery is scarce. Many farmers use a 'walking tractor', a small-engined cultivator which is guided by hand, like a lawn-mower. In many regions water buffalo are still used for farm work.

Villages used to be organised into communes, whose members shared all the farm work. Today the government allows some independent farmers to work the land. The farmers agree to supply a certain amount of food to the cities but may sell any extra produce at their local market.

In the towns and cities, China's factories are still mostly state-owned, but some are run as private companies.

Special Economic Zones have been set

Lessons in a village primary school

up since the 1980s in the hope that foreign businesses will bring money and new technology into China. Some foreign goods are imported, but they are expensive and many people cannot afford to buy them.

In most families, both men and women go out to work. Women are an important part of the Chinese labour force and receive equal pay with men. Women work on farms and in the army, in factories, shops, hospitals, schools and hotels.

Tourism and communications

Tourism is now a major industry in China. Visitors come from all over the world. Many arrive in China from Hong Kong. Others fly into Beijing.

There are many local flights in China and each major city has an airport. China has a huge road network, but most highways give a rough and bumpy ride!

Working for health

One major health problem is caused by smoking. The Chinese grow tobacco and are among the heaviest smokers in the world.

There are modern hospitals in China's towns and cities, and small clinics in country areas. Many people take the natural Chinese medicines which have been used for centuries. Most of these are made up from herbs, flowers, roots and bark.

Another traditional cure is acupuncture. Fine needles are placed in the patient's body at special points. He or she soon feels healthy and relaxed.

Acupuncture keeps patients in good health.

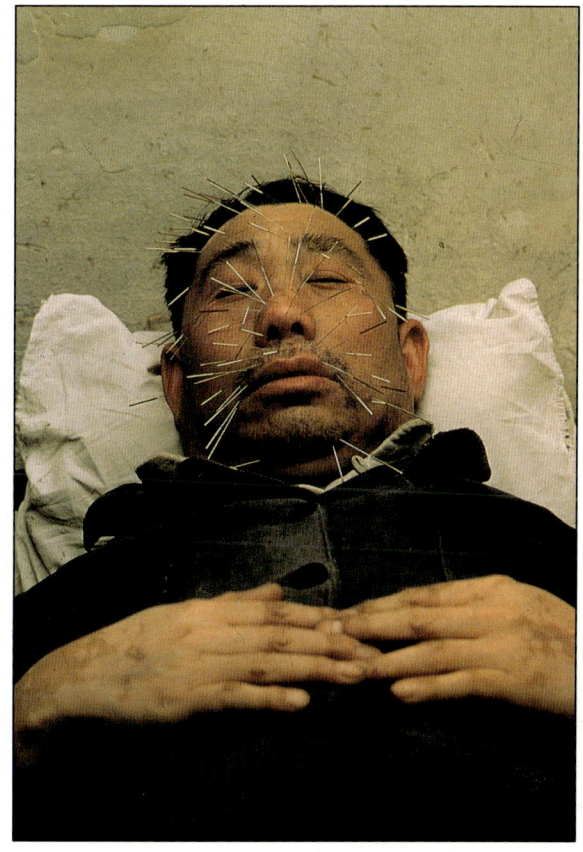

At home

Houses and flats in China are often very crowded. Kitchens, courtyards and the water supply may be shared with other families. Housing conditions in China are similar to those in many other Asian countries, but they are poor by European and American standards.

In recent years though there has been a great increase in the number of families with refrigerators, washing machines, sewing machines and televisions. Many people gather to watch television in public places, such as tea houses or bars.

Chinese families often live together, with the grandparents looking after the smallest children during the day, while the parents are out working.

China's population is growing very quickly. There are over 44 000 births each day. The government expects parents who live in the cities to keep their families small. Parents' lives are made much easier if they agree to have only one child. Some people complain that single children in China today are being spoiled by over-loving parents.

Flats and courtyards in Datong, a large mining town in Shanxi province

A Chinese family sits down to dinner.

However action of some kind has to be taken to control the birthrate.

Mealtime in China

The day starts early. Breakfast may be a quick meal of rice or noodles. The midday or evening meal is often based on rice or noodles too. The meal may be served with fresh vegetables such as greens, peppers, spring onions or mushrooms. Sometimes there may be delicious pork, chicken, freshwater fish or seafood. Soup is served at the end of a meal rather than at the beginning.

Chopsticks are normally used rather than knives and forks. Most meals are eaten at home, although people in towns sometimes eat out in restaurants.

Popular street snacks include pancakes, dumplings, hard-boiled eggs, sweet buns and ice cream. Tea is drunk with all meals, and beer is popular. A special occasion may be toasted in *maotai*, a very strong alcoholic drink made from sorghum.

Around the regions

Some Chinese food may seem very strange to outsiders, but most people agree that Chinese dishes are among the finest in the world. The delicate tastes vary from region to region.

- Beijing is famous for its crispy duck. Northern cooking uses a lot of sweet bean sauce, sesame oil and garlic.
- Eastern Chinese cooking uses very light sauces. The region is known for tender Zhejiang ham, fresh fish and vegetarian dishes.
- Sichuan cooking is the spiciest and hottest in China, using local peppercorns, chili, peanuts, garlic and ginger.
- Cantonese cooking, from Guangdong and Hong Kong, includes dishes such as sweet-and-sour pork and trays of tasty snacks known as *dim sum*.
- Inner Mongolia is famous for its lamb dishes. The meat is simmered and dipped into sauces at the table.
- Tibetans eat *tsampa*, which is roasted barley flour mixed with tea and rancid yak's butter.

A stall sells snacks in Chongqing.

Leisure and the arts

In 1990 the Asian Games were held in Beijing. China had become one of the world's great sporting nations. Popular sports include swimming, athletics, table tennis, basket ball, volleyball, gymnastics and football. Traditional sports in more remote regions include wrestling, archery and horseriding.

In city parks people of all ages like to keep fit. Some go jogging, or do exercises to taped music. Others gather at dawn to practise the graceful movements of *taijiquan*, known overseas as 'tai chi'. China is famous for its ancient martial arts, such as *gongfu* ('kung fu').

Parks are meeting places too, for people playing open-air board games, Chinese chess or cards. Many people fly paper kites. Some of these are in the shape of beautiful birds or butterflies. Young city dwellers enjoy dancing and discos. They like to buy tapes of their favourite pop groups.

Festivals and holidays

The dates of many of China's ancient festivals are set by the position of the Moon, so they fall on different days each year.

'Tai chi' exercises in Shanghai

Dragon dancers welcome in the spring.

The Spring Festival, sometimes called the Chinese New Year, starts on the day of the first new moon after 21 January. It is the chief holiday of the year, a time for family reunions, weddings and feasting. Dancers weave through the streets with a long paper dragon. Other festivals include the Lantern Festival and the Festival of Clear Brightness in spring, the Dragon Boat Festival in summer and the Mid-Autumn Festival.

Modern holidays include Women's Day (8 March), Labour Day (1 May), Children's Day (1 June) and China's National Day (1 October).

Music, arts and crafts

China's classical music developed at the court of the emperors, while its folk music developed in the countryside. Operas, in which people sing and act, are very popular. The actors paint their faces and wear colourful costumes. They play the parts of heroes, princesses and villains. Theatres also put on shows of conjuring and acrobatics.

For thousands of years China has produced wonderful landscape paintings, as well as metalwork and carvings in a green stone called jade. The Chinese were the first to discover the secrets of making beautiful silk and fine porcelain.

The art of writing

Poetry and writing are at the centre of Chinese life. Painting and literature come together in an art called calligraphy. The Chinese language is written with thousands of symbols, called characters. Each one is beautifully painted with a brush and ink. A poem is meant to be looked at, as well as read. It may be hung on the wall.

An actress plays the part of a warrior in this traditional Chinese opera.

China long ago

People have lived in China since prehistoric times. The earliest remains of human ancestors have been found at Lantian, in the northern province of Shaanxi. They date back to about 600 000 BC. Remains found in a cave at Zhoukoudian, near Beijing, belonged to people who used fire and stone tools. They are over 400 000 years old.

From about 7000 BC people began to settle around the Yellow River. They hunted and fished and then learned how to farm. On the edge of the city of Xi'an, at Banpo, visitors can see a farming village which was built about 5000 years ago. The villagers grew millet, raised animals and made pottery in kilns.

Historians divide China's ancient history up into the periods when it was ruled by a particular royal family. These periods are called dynasties. China's first dynasty was called the Xia. It is dated to about 1800 BC, but this is a period of myths and legends. Little is known for certain about this period of history.

The Shang dynasty, which ruled from about 1480 to 1122 BC, built towns. These people knew how to make silk and bronze, a metal mixed from copper and tin. They also used a form of writing.

The Zhou came from the north of China and overthrew Shang rule in 1122 BC. Their rulers, like China's later emperors, called themselves the 'Sons of Heaven'.

Two great teachers lived in these times. Lao Zi (Lao Tse) was born in about 604 BC and Kong Fuzi (Confucius) in 551 BC. Their ideas about how people should behave were later to become the basis of new religions, called Taoism and Confucianism.

A man-and-tiger vessel from the Shang period

The underground army of Qin Shi Huangdi

A buried army

About 2500 years ago China consisted of small states which were frequently at war with each other. Their weapons were made of iron. The country was finally united in 221 BC, under the emperor Qin Shi Huangdi. He was buried near Xi'an, surrounded by thousands of lifelike soldiers made of bronze or terracotta (fired clay). This underground 'army' guarded his tomb from 210 BC until its discovery in 1974.

The Great Wall

Work on the Great Wall of China was begun over 2300 years ago. For well over a thousand years slaves, soldiers and peasants were sent north to work on the wall. The purpose of the wall was to protect China from attack. It also served as a road and a trading route.

Trains entering China from Mongolia today pass through a gap in the wall to the north of Beijing. The wall can be seen zig-zagging its way up and down the mountain valleys, as far as the eye can see. Its main section is about 3460 km (2162 miles) long, but side branches make up nearly the same length again. The total may once have been as much as 10 000 km (6250 miles).

A vast empire

In the 400 years after China became one country, it grew into a vast empire, under the Han dynasty. It traded with the outside world. The Buddhist religion was brought to China, from India at this time. This was also an age of new ideas and technical inventions.

China's Great Wall can be seen from the Moon!

The Middle Kingdom

The Chinese call their country *Zhongguo*, which means the 'Middle Kingdom'. For centuries they saw themselves as being at the centre of the world, surrounded on all sides by foreigners who knew little about civilization.

For much of their history, this was true. There were long periods of war, but during the period that Europeans call the Middle Ages, China was the most advanced country in the world.

This was the time of the Tang (AD 618-906) and the Song (AD 960-1279) dynasties. Printing was invented at this time and calendars and dictionaries were published.

During the 1200s China was invaded by fierce Mongol horsemen, but the new rulers soon picked up Chinese ways. The land ruled by the Mongol emperor of China, Kublai Khan, stretched right across Asia. His capital was Khanbalik, on the site of modern Beijing. Foreign explorers such as Marco Polo, from Venice, marvelled at the splendour of the Chinese court.

An old painting shows Marco Polo at the court of Kublai Khan.

British ships attack the Chinese fleet in 1841.

From 1368 until 1644 the country was ruled by southerners, the Ming. Porcelain and silks were exported far and wide, and fleets of Chinese ships travelled to Southeast Asia and Africa.

Foreigners and rebels

In 1644 power passed to the Manchu people, from China's northeast. Their dynasty, the Qing, was to be the last. Outside China, the world was changing fast.

Portuguese ships were already using China's trading routes. The British, who had seized control of India, were selling Indian opium to the Chinese. The Chinese did their best to prevent the trade, but the British refused to stop selling the opium. In 1839 China began a series of wars with Britain. In the end China was forced to give up land – including Hong Kong.

Many more foreign countries began to set up trading posts in China. French, Germans and Americans walked the streets of Shanghai. Christian missionaries travelled up the Chang Jiang. Russia and Japan hoped to seize land ruled by China.

China was no longer a great power and many of its people blamed their rulers. In 1853 rebels captured the city of Nanjing, but many were killed with the help of foreign troops. In 1900 foreign troops again put down a rebellion, in Beijing.

The great empress

During these troubled times, some of the emperors who came to throne were children. The real power in the land was the regent, who ruled in their place. The Empress Cixi ruled China as regent. She was a powerful and ruthless woman, but she could not control the foreign nations who were breaking up her country. She died in 1908. The last emperor of all was a small boy, Puyi, who ruled until 1911.

The Empress Cixi in 1903

New worlds

In 1911 there was yet another rebellion, in Wuchang. It was successful and brought an end to thousands of years of rule by emperors. China now became a republic. Its new leader was Dr Sun Yatsen, from Guangzhou. He wanted to modernise the country, but the following year he was forced to hand over power to a warlord called Yuan Shikai.

In the early 1920s a revolutionary movement started whose aim was to create a modern China which would be free from foreign control. The Nationalist party, called the Guomindang, and the Chinese Communist Party led this revolutionary movement. There was an uneasy alliance between the two parties. However in 1925 a new leader took over the Guomindang. His name was Chiang Kai-Shek (Jiang Jieshi).

Mao Zedong leads his fighters through the mountains in 1947. He was a brilliant guerrilla leader.

For many years he tried to crush the Communists, but the Communists were successful and well-organised fighters.

During the 1930s the Japanese launched an invasion of China and from 1941-5 this conflict became part of the Second World War. The Chinese formed a United Front, but it soon collapsed. The Communists had to fight both the Guomindang and the Japanese.

These were hard years and many people starved. Japan was defeated, but it was three more years before peace came to China. In 1949 the communist forces finally defeated Chiang Kai-Shek and his nationalists, who fled to the island of Taiwan.

Red Guards in Tiananmen Square during the Cultural Revolution

Communism in China

October 1949 saw the beginning of the new People's Republic of China. The Communists brought in many reforms. Land was given back to the peasants and heavy industry was developed. Mao Zedong called this the 'Great Leap Forward'. There were many achievements, but also many failures.

During the 1960s Mao Zedong's picture was displayed everywhere and everyone studied his writings. Young people called Red Guards were encouraged to attack anyone who held ideas that were thought to be old-fashioned or foreign-influenced. Many people suffered during this period, which was known as the 'Cultural Revolution'.

Today and tomorrow

Mao Zedong died in 1976 and his chief supporters, called the 'Gang of Four', soon lost power. Under the leadership of Deng Xiaoping, China opened its doors to the outside world once more. The old ideas of Mao were given up one by one. The Chinese government said it still wanted to create a communist state, but that it was going to do so by other means. To many, the reforms looked like capitalism. The streets were now filled with advertisements for Japanese watches and American soft drinks rather than political posters. There were calls for changes. Some people wanted more say in how they were governed. In 1989 many students calling for democracy were killed by soldiers in Tiananmen Square, Beijing.

Most of China's leaders are now old men. What will China's future be in the twenty-first century?

Advertisements appear on the streets of Beijing.

Fact file

Flag and anthem

The Chinese flag is red, the colour of revolution. Its large yellow star stands for communism. Its four smaller stars stand for unity.

The national emblem shows the Tiananmen Gate of Beijing's Forbidden City.

China's national anthem is *The March of the Volunteers*, composed by Nie Er in 1935.

Money

The Chinese currency is called *Renminbi* ('people's money'). One *yuan* is made up of 10 *jiao* or 100 *fen*.

Religion

China has no official religion. During the Cultural Revolution temples and churches were closed down, but today people may worship once again. Many Chinese religious beliefs come from Taoism and Confucianism. China has many Buddhists as well as followers of the Islamic and Christian faiths.

Education

There are only two terms in the Chinese school year. Children go to toddlers' classes and then to primary school. At 13 they go on to 'junior middle school'. At 16 they may go on to 'senior middle school' and college, take up a training course, or start work.

Chinese writing

The Chinese language is written in a script made up of about 50 000 different characters! About 5000 of these are in everyday use. A way of writing Chinese words in the western alphabet is sometimes used. This is called *Pinyin*.

The media

The main Chinese newspaper is called *The People's Daily*. English-speakers can catch up on local news in the *China Daily*. Chinese television has one national channel, which carries advertisements. Each of the provinces and regions has its own channel. Cinemas are popular in every Chinese city.

Inventions

Many things that we now take for granted were invented in China. They include paper, silk, magnetic compasses, porcelain, gunpowder, fireworks, printing, clockwork, and a machine to warn of earthquakes.

Chinese astrology

Traditionally each new year in China is named after an animal. 1994 is the year of the Dog. 1995 is the Pig, 1996 the Rat, 1997 the Ox, 1998 the Tiger, 1999 the Rabbit, 2000 the Dragon, 2001 the Snake, 2002 the Horse, 2003 the Goat, 2004 the Monkey and 2005 the Cockerel.

Some famous people

Lao Tse (b c604 BC) was a librarian and philosopher

Confucius (551-479 BC) was a court official and philosopher

Qu Yuan (c340-278 BC) was a poet

Qin Shi Huangdi (d210 BC) was the emperor of the first united China

Sima Qian (d90 BC) was an historian

Tang Taozi (d AD 649) was an emperor who defeated Tibetans and Turks

Yan Liben (d 673) was a painter

Wu (d705) was an empress who supported Buddhism

Wang Wei (699-759) was a painter

Du Fu (d 770) was a poet

Kublai Khan (1215-94) was a Mongol emperor of China

Zheng He (1400s) was an admiral and navigator

Kangxi (1654-1722) was an emperor who supported scholarship and the arts

Cao Xuequin (d1763) was a novelist

Cixi (1835-1908) was an empress and powerful regent

Sun Yatsen (1866-1925) was the founder of the Chinese republic

Lu Xun (1881-1936) was a leading author

Chiang Kai-Shek (1887-1975) was president of China (1928-31 and 1943-49)

Mao Zedong (1893-1976) was chairman of the Chinese Communist Party (1949-1976)

Deng Xiaoping (1904 -) is a politician and statesman

Li Peng (1928-) became the premier of China in 1988

Some key events in history

7000 BC Farming started in northern China

1122 BC the Shang dynasty was overthrown

300 BC work on the Great Wall started

221 BC China became one country under Qin Shi Huangdi

AD **65** Buddhism arrived in China

220 the end of the Han dynasty

960 the start of the Song dynasty

1215 Mongols attacked China

1260 Kublai Khan became emperor

1368 the start of the Ming dynasty

1408 2000 scholars completed an encyclopedia of 11 095 volumes

1421 Beijing became the capital of China

1644 the Manchu invaded China

1839 First Opium War between China and Britain

1850-64 Taiping Rebellion

1856 Second Opium War

1899-1900 Boxer Rebellion

1911 Sun Yatsen's republic ended the rule of the emperors

1921 the Communist Party was founded

1937-45 the War of Resistance against Japan

1946-49 the Chinese Civil War

1949 the People's Republic of China was founded

1958 Mao's 'Great Leap Forward'

1966-69 the Cultural Revolution

1971 China joined the United Nations

1976 Mao Zedong died

1977 Deng Xiaoping became vice-premier

1989 Tiananmen Square massacre

Index

acupuncture 19
airports 19
arts 23

Beijing 11, 16, 17, 19, 21, 22, 24, 25, 26, 27, 29, 30
Buddhism 8, 14, 17, 25, 30, 31

Chang Jiang 10, 11, 12, 27
Chiang Kai-Shek 28, 31
Chongqing 10, 11
communism 7, 17, 28, 29, 30, 31
Cultural Revolution 29, 30, 31

Deng Xiaoping 29, 31

education 30

farming 10, 12, 18, 19, 24, 31
festivals 22, 23
fishing 6
food 18, 21
Forbidden City 17, 30
forestry 15

Grand Canal 11
Great Wall 25, 31
Guangzhou 5, 6, 11, 28

Han Chinese 5, 14
Hong Kong 7, 19, 21, 27
Huang He (Yellow River) 12, 24
Hunan 11

industry 6, 11, 13, 15, 18, 19, 29
Inner Mongolia 14, 21
invention 25, 26, 30

kites 22
Kunming 7

lacquer 6
languages 5, 8, 23, 30

Macao 7
Manchuria 15
Manchus 27, 31
Mao Zedong 17, 29, 31

martial arts 22
medicine 19
Miao 5
Ming dynasty 27, 31
money 30
Mongols 5, 14, 26, 31
music 23

oil 9, 15
opera 23

pandas 10
population 5, 20
porcelain 6, 23, 27, 30
prehistory 24

Qing dynasty 27

railways 7, 13, 16, 25
religion 14, 24, 30
rice 6, 11, 18, 21

Shang dynasty 24, 31
Shanghai 11, 17, 27
Sichuan 10, 21
silk 6, 9, 23, 27, 30
Song dynasty 26, 31
sport 22

Taiwan 7, 28
Tang dynasty 26
tea 6, 9, 21
Terracotta Army 25
Tiananmen Square 17, 29, 30, 31
Tianjin 13, 17
Tibet 8, 9, 21
tourism 6, 19

wildlife reserves 10, 15
writing 23, 30

Xia dynasty 24

Yunnan 7

Zhou dynasty 24